California's
Spanish
Missions

Lisa Greathouse and Ted Fauce

Consultants

Kristina Jovin, M.A.T.
Alvord Unified School District
Teacher of the Year

Vanessa Ann Gunther, Ph.D.
Department of History
Chapman University

Publishing Credits

Rachelle Cracchiolo, M.S.Ed., *Publisher*
Conni Medina, M.A.Ed., *Managing Editor*
Emily R. Smith, M.A.Ed., *Series Developer*
June Kikuchi, *Content Director*
Marc Pioch, M.A.Ed., and Susan Daddis, M.A.Ed., *Editors*
Courtney Roberson, *Senior Graphic Designer*

Image Credits: p.4 Library of Congress [g3291s.mf000074]; p.5 Perry-Castañeda Library Map Collection; pp.6–7 Private Collection/J. T. Vintage/Bridgeman Images; p.7 (bottom) Copyright © NativeStock/North Wind Picture Archives; pp.8–9 Photo by Morton Kunstler/National Geographic/Getty Images; p.12 (top) Photo by Stephen Bay; p.13 (bottom) Diary of Gaspar de Portolá During the California Expedition of 1769-1770 edited by Donald Eugene Smith and Frederick John Teggart; pp.14–15 Illustration © Teacher Created Materials; pp.17, 25 California Missions Resource Center, 2016, www.missionscalifornia.com; pp.18–19 Granger, NYC; p.20 California Historical Society Collections at the Autry/Bridgeman Images; p.21 Courtesy of the California History Room, California State Library, Sacramento, California; pp.22–23, 29 (bottom) North Wind Picture Archives; p.24 Bettman/Getty Images; p.32 Photo by Morton Kunstler/National Geographic/Getty Images; all other images from iStock and/or Shutterstock.

Library of Congress Cataloging-in-Publication Data

Names: Greathouse, Lisa E., author. | Fauce, Ted, author.
Title: California's Spanish missions / Lisa Greathouse and Ted Fauce.
Description: Huntington Beach, CA : Teacher Created Materials, 2018. |
   Includes index. | Audience: Grades 4-6.
Identifiers: LCCN 2017014091 (print) | LCCN 2017019038 (ebook) | ISBN
   9781425835040 (eBook) | ISBN 9781425832346 (pbk.)
Subjects: LCSH: Spanish mission buildings--California--History--Juvenile
   literature. | Indians of North
   America--Missions--California--History--Juvenile literature. |
   California--History--To 1846--Juvenile literature.
Classification: LCC F864 (ebook) | LCC F864 .G785 2018 (print) | DDC
   979.4/01--dc23

LC record available at https://lccn.loc.gov/2017014091

Teacher Created Materials

5301 Oceanus Drive
Huntington Beach, CA 92649-1030
http://www.tcmpub.com

ISBN 978-1-4258-3234-6

Table of Contents

A New World 4

The Sacred Mission. 8

Mission Buildings 14

Mission Life: Changes and Conflicts 20

Legacy of the Missions 26

Track It! 28

Glossary 30

Index 31

Your Turn! 32

kitchen at Mission Santa Barbara

A New World

In 1492, Christopher Columbus set sail for Asia. He was searching for a quicker route to the spices, silk, and art that could be found there. What he found was a new world. It became known as the Americas.

Soon, explorers claimed huge pieces of this new land. They wanted to start **colonies**. Spain, Portugal, England, and France fought for control of the New World. They wanted to find gold, silver, and jewels. These resources were used to expand power and influence. But riches and trade were not the only reasons to explore the new land.

Sharing America

People in Europe wanted to spread their religions to the world. Spain felt that religion could improve the lives of the native people living in the Americas. Spanish leaders also saw this as a way to protect and grow its power in the New World.

P A C

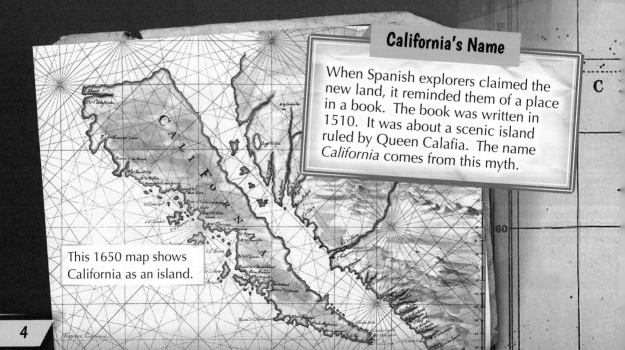

This 1650 map shows California as an island.

California's Name

When Spanish explorers claimed the new land, it reminded them of a place in a book. The book was written in 1510. It was about a scenic island ruled by Queen Calafia. The name *California* comes from this myth.

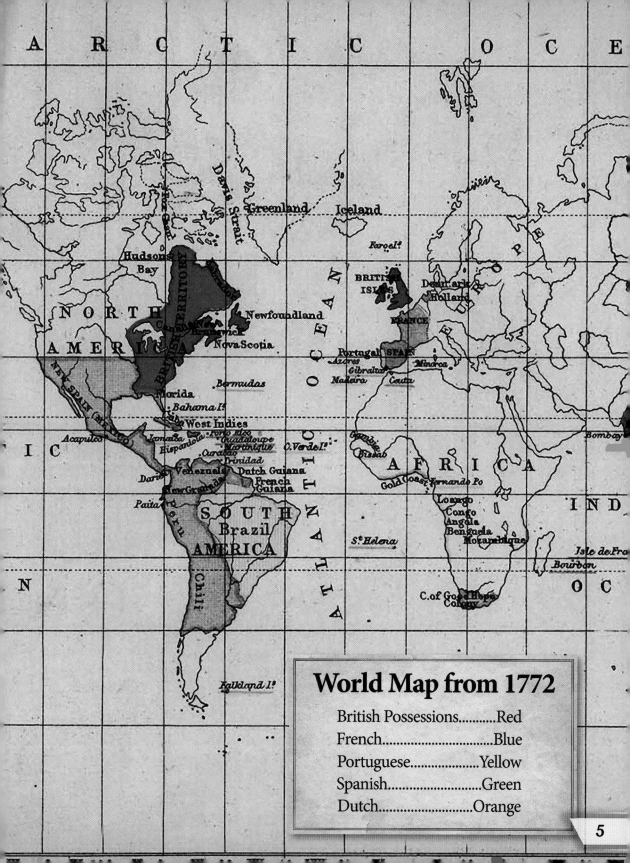

ARCTIC OCEAN

Davis Strait

Greenland   Iceland

Faroe I?

Hudson's Bay

BRITISH ISLES

Denmark & Holland

NORTH AMERICA

BRITISH TERRITORY

Canada
New Brunswick
Nova Scotia

Newfoundland

FRANCE

Portugal SPAIN
Azores
Gibraltar
Madeira   Ceuta
Minorca

NEW SPAIN (MEXICO)

Bermudas

Florida
Bahama I?
West Indies

Acapulco   Jamaica   Porto Rico
Hispaniola   Guadaloupe
Curacao   Martinique   C. Verde I?

EUROPE

Bombay

Cape Verd

Gambia
Bissao

AFRICA

IND

Darien   Venezuela   Dutch Guiana
New Granada   French Guiana

Gold Coast   Fernando Po

Paita

PERU

SOUTH Brazil AMERICA

St. Helena

Loango
Congo
Angola
Benguela
Mozambique

Isle de Fra

Bourbon

Chili

C. of Good Hope Colony

OC

N

Falkland I?

World Map from 1772

British Possessions...........Red
French..............................Blue
Portuguese....................Yellow
Spanish.........................Green
Dutch............................Orange

5

When settlers came to the New World they saw millions of people living there. These people were American Indians. They had lived on this land for thousands of years. Their ancestors had come to North America in the last Ice Age. At that time, Russia and Alaska were joined by a land bridge. Once they crossed the land bridge, they spread through the continent and formed tribes.

California Indians lived in what is now California and northern Mexico. These tribes lived off the land. Their homes, clothes, and even their food were based on where they lived. Tribes near the coast mainly ate sea creatures, such as otters and seals. Many tribes in the valleys lived off birds, such as quail.

These different ways of life built a huge trade network. Food was one of the most common things for tribes to trade. Each tribe traded items from their area for things they needed from tribes in other areas. When settlers arrived, they found tribes that were independent but **interrelated**.

American Indians in Yosemite Valley

An Appetite for Acorns

Since acorns were plentiful in the state, they were a large part of the California Indians' diet. Preparing the nuts was a long process. First, acorns were dried for a year. Then, grinding tools were used to make them into meal. This is similar to flour. After the meal was made, some tribes used it to make biscuits or bread. Others boiled the meal and ate the mush, which is thicker than a soup.

Strong Homes

California Indians used different materials to build their houses. Tribes living close to the coast built grass mat houses. If tribes lived in an area with lots of trees, they built their houses out of cedar bark (shown here).

The Sacred Mission

Spanish leaders knew that **missions** helped settle and protect their land. They had built missions in Florida and Texas years before. In California, they planned to do the same thing. Men who were loyal to Spain were needed. These men had to be willing to die for their faith. The priests knew it was their duty to **convert** the American Indians in California. Soldiers had to secure the land for Spain. This became known as the *Sacred Expedition*.

The Franciscan Order

An *order* is a name used for a group of religious men. Many priests who came to America to build missions belonged to the Spanish Franciscan Order. These priests agreed to live simple lives and didn't own property. This allowed them to focus on converting the native people.

The journey began in 1769. A group of men went to San Diego on horseback and by foot. There were soldiers and priests in the group. Gaspar de Portolá (deh por-toh-LAH) led the soldiers. Father Junípero (hoo-NEE-peh-roh) Serra led the priests. One man kept a journal of the trip and the land. His name was Father Juan Crespí (crehs-PEE). His journal provides a lot of information.

Keeping Records

Crespí wrote about mountains, valleys, trees, and animals. He noted how American Indians lived. His notes came in handy for the men who built the missions.

Geography

The Spanish explored all the way to the San Francisco Bay.

Junípero Serra

Father Serra is the most well-known priest of the Mission Era. He wanted to be more than just a priest. His goal was to bring his religion to the American Indians. After he started the first mission in San Diego, he helped build eight more.

Serra was very strict. He converted thousands of American Indians. He forced them to adopt a new way of life. Soldiers helped enforce his stern rules. Near the end of his life, Serra had plans for more missions. After he died, his followers helped finish what he had planned. The last mission in San Francisco was opened in 1823. In all, it took 54 years to build 21 missions.

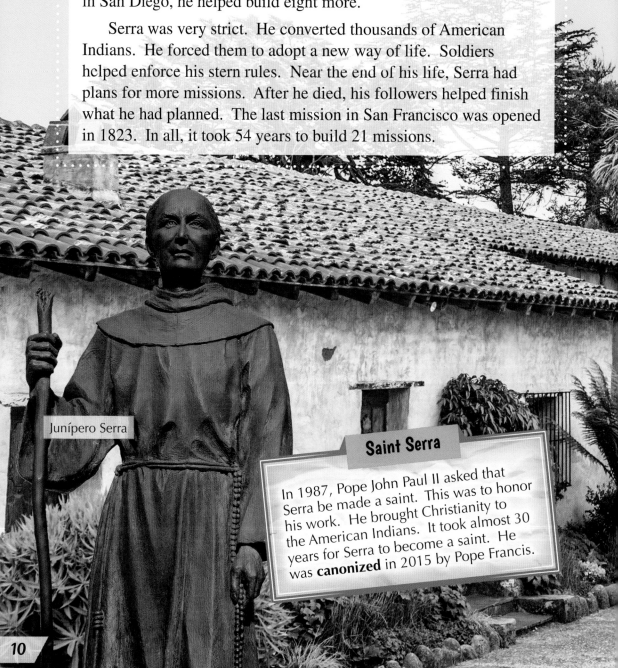

Junípero Serra

Saint Serra

In 1987, Pope John Paul II asked that Serra be made a saint. This was to honor his work. He brought Christianity to the American Indians. It took almost 30 years for Serra to become a saint. He was **canonized** in 2015 by Pope Francis.

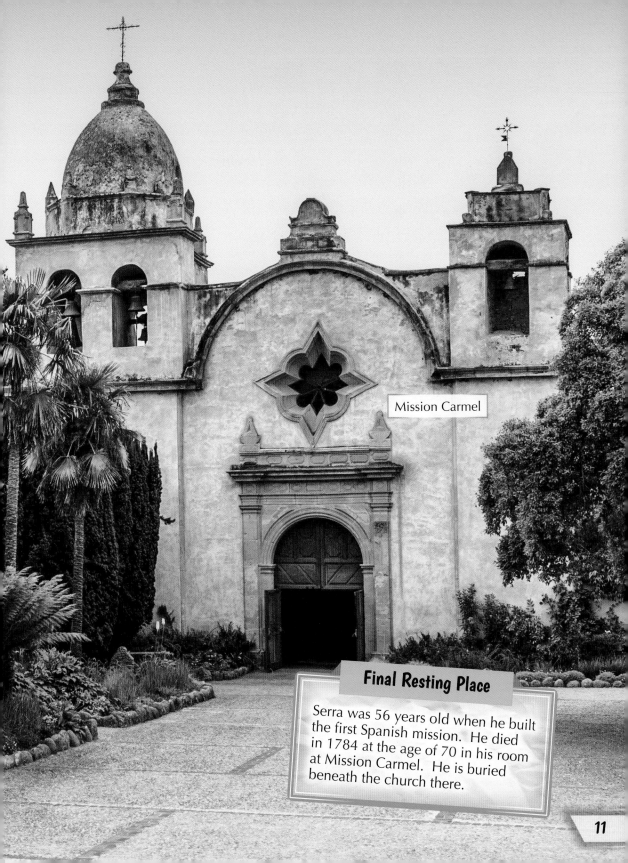

Mission Carmel

Final Resting Place

Serra was 56 years old when he built the first Spanish mission. He died in 1784 at the age of 70 in his room at Mission Carmel. He is buried beneath the church there.

Gaspar de Portolá

The Royal Road

Portolá's route north through California became known as *El Camino Real*. This means "The King's Road." Today, Highway 101 (shown here) follows much of this same route.

Gaspar de Portolá

Many people helped build the missions and keep them safe. Portolá was one of those men. He was a Spanish army captain. In 1767, he sailed to the New World. He joined Father Serra on the Sacred Expedition. He helped build the **presidios**. These buildings protected the missions.

The trip was hard. Along the way, the Spanish experienced earthquakes and often ran out of food. When the food supply was low, the Spanish traded with the American Indians. The soldiers traded beads and their clothes. In return, they received fish and corn.

Portolá trekked north to San Francisco. He went as far as where the Golden Gate Bridge now stands. He helped Spain keep California. At the time, Spanish leaders feared that Russian fur trappers would claim this land. Portolá set the groundwork for missions to be **founded**. The success of his journey relied on the help of American Indians. Sadly, these same missions would change the native peoples' lives and culture.

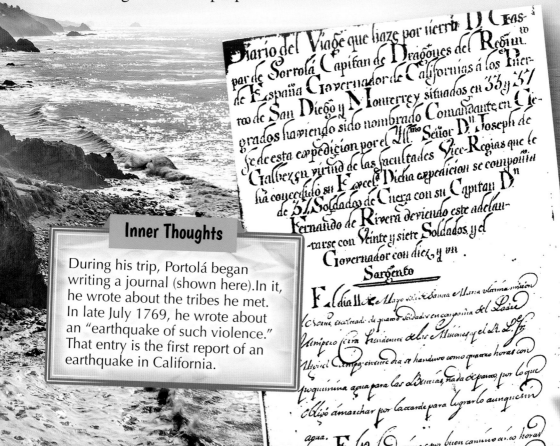

Inner Thoughts

During his trip, Portolá began writing a journal (shown here). In it, he wrote about the tribes he met. In late July 1769, he wrote about an "earthquake of such violence." That entry is the first report of an earthquake in California.

Mission Buildings

Each mission had many buildings surrounded by land that had been cleared of trees. Many missions were built on hills. All of them had churches and buildings where the priests and soldiers lived. Each had a kitchen, a dining hall, classrooms, and workshops. There were also large pieces of land to grow crops, as well as **corrals** and coops for animals.

American Indian village

To be safe, some missions were built inside presidios surrounded by strong walls. Other missions were on land called **ranchos**. The ranchos were used for raising cattle and sheep. Some missions became the center of villages known as *pueblos*. This is where many people lived together. In later years, many pueblos would become larger cities.

laundry area

gardens

Unique Architecture

All missions are noted for their use of domes, vaults, and arches. The most distinctive part of each mission church is the **belfry**. The *campanile* (kam-puh-NEE-lee) style belfry was a large tower that held one or more bells.

church

15

Differences Among Missions

Missions were not all the same. One of the reasons for this is California's geography. The state is long and has many miles of land near the ocean. Because of the state's size, shape, and location, it has varied **climates**. Rain and snow fall mostly on the mountains. This process makes the land behind them dry. These areas form deserts. Mountains and deserts were not good places to build missions.

Most missions were built along the coast, which has a mild climate. Life in a mild climate is easier. It's great for raising crops and animals.

Each mission relied on nearby natural resources. The **missionaries** learned how to use those resources from the California Indians. The mission system settled and developed the land for Spain.

Inland Mission

The mission that was built farthest from the coast was Soledad Mission. It is 30 miles (48 kilometers) inland from the coast.

Geography

SOLEDAD MISSION

FOUNDED   RESTORATION
OCT. 9, 1791   OCT. 9, 1955

Mission to Mission

The builders of the missions wanted to keep in touch. They built each mission about one day's horseback ride apart. Landforms, fresh water sources, and other factors also determined where the missions were built. Most missions were about 30 miles (48 kilometers) apart.

Geography

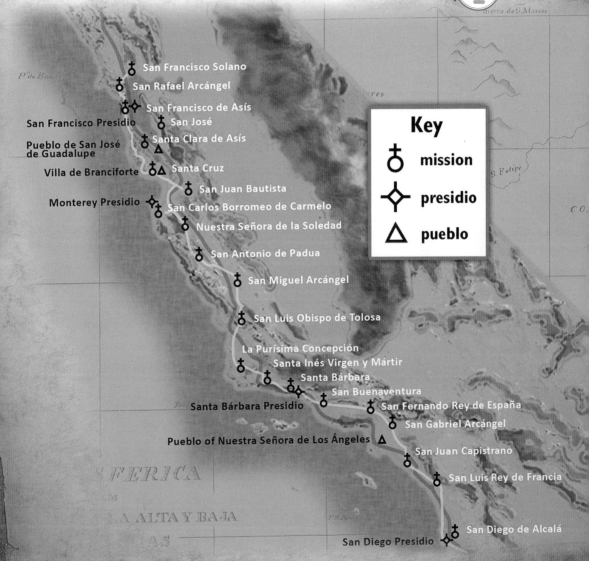

San Francisco Solano

San Rafael Arcángel

San Francisco de Asís

San Francisco Presidio   San José

Pueblo de San José de Guadalupe   Santa Clara de Asís

Villa de Branciforte   Santa Cruz

San Juan Bautista

Monterey Presidio   San Carlos Borromeo de Carmelo

Nuestra Señora de la Soledad

San Antonio de Padua

San Miguel Arcángel

San Luis Obispo de Tolosa

La Purísima Concepción

Santa Inés Virgen y Mártir

Santa Bárbara

San Buenaventura

Santa Bárbara Presidio   San Fernando Rey de España

San Gabriel Arcángel

Pueblo of Nuestra Señora de Los Ángeles

San Juan Capistrano

San Luis Rey de Francia

San Diego de Alcalá

San Diego Presidio

Key

⚥ mission

◇ presidio

△ pueblo

San Luis Obispo

Mission San Luis Obispo was very different from the other missions. It was founded in 1772 by Father Serra. It was built in an area that had a lot of grizzly bears. The mission relied on the meat that the bears could provide. Food was running low at other missions. There was a large hunt. Many bears were killed, and the meat was shared. Later, people began farming wheat and corn to provide food.

Weather Matters

Missions in the southern part of California had much different weather from those in the north. The south was sunny but dry. Citrus fruits grew well in the south.

Geography

Mission Santa Clara, 1849

Santa Clara

Mission Santa Clara was one of the nine missions built by Father Serra. It was built in 1777. Flooding from the local river made the soil wet, similar to a **marsh**. Over the next 45 years, this mission had to be moved more than once. The mission was moved to its final place in 1822. The soil in the area was very good for farming. Santa Clara had one of the best wheat crops of all the missions. Like many missions in the north, people at Santa Clara grew grapes and made wine.

From Mission to College

Santa Clara University opened in 1851. It was built on the site of the old mission. It is the oldest college in the state. Today, students can see parts of the old mission's buildings around campus.

Mission Life: Changes and Conflicts

People lived in the area that is now California for thousands of years. Pieces of clay pots and weapons from these times have been found. Before the missions were built, American Indians followed their own **traditions**. More than 50 tribes lived there. They spoke over 100 different languages. They had thriving villages and knew how to live off the land.

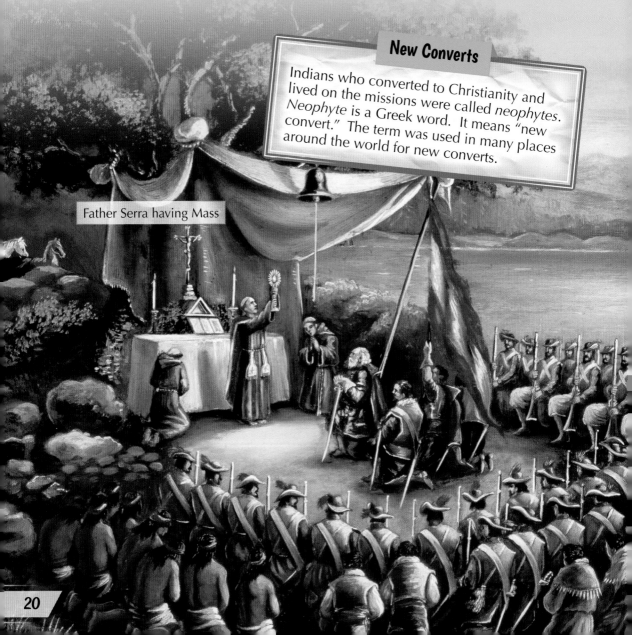

New Converts

Indians who converted to Christianity and lived on the missions were called *neophytes*. *Neophyte* is a Greek word. It means "new convert." The term was used in many places around the world for new converts.

Father Serra having Mass

For the American Indians, mission life was a change from their previous lives. The Spanish forced them to live and work at the missions. Their children went to schools there, too. They learned a new language and had to convert to a new religion. Many native people fought against these changes to their way of life.

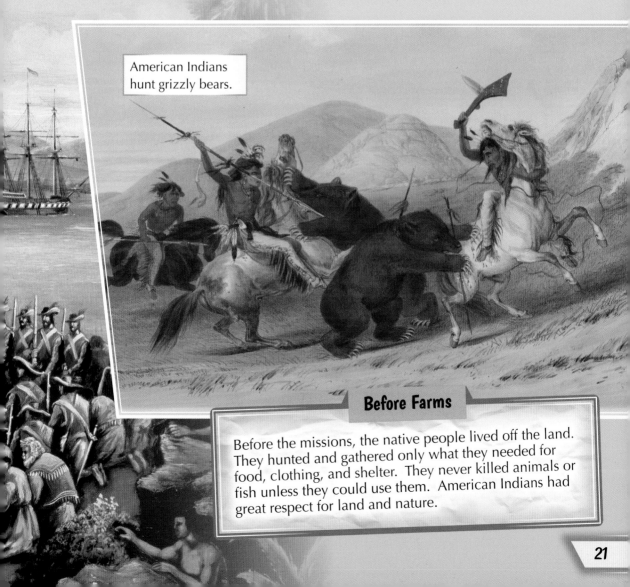

American Indians hunt grizzly bears.

Before Farms

Before the missions, the native people lived off the land. They hunted and gathered only what they needed for food, clothing, and shelter. They never killed animals or fish unless they could use them. American Indians had great respect for land and nature.

Changes

Mission lands were split into sections. Some of the land was used for growing crops. Other parts were used for raising animals. All the land needed to be cleared of rocks, trees, and weeds to make room for crops and animals. American Indians did this hard work at the missions all day long. Many native people tried to flee. One in ten ran away from the missions. Many more tried to leave but were stopped. If they were caught, they were forced to return to the missions.

soldiers, priests, and California Indians at one of the missions

Leaving was risky but so was staying. When Europeans came to the New World, they brought illnesses with them. The native people did not have **immunities**. In 1806, measles spread throughout the missions. It killed more than 1,000 American Indians at the Santa Barbara mission alone. Most of those who died were children. During this time, 60,000 American Indians would die at the missions. Many of those deaths were caused by disease.

Culture Survives

Today, California is home to the largest number of native people in the country. There are over 100 tribes in the state. These tribes have played key roles in saving forests and animals in the state. They have also worked to keep their culture alive.

Civics

Conflicts

Not all American Indians tried to flee from the missions. Some tried to resist their new way of life. There were many **revolts**. In 1775, nearly 1,000 native people attacked the San Diego mission. They burned it to the ground. During the night, a priest was killed. Spanish soldiers caught and punished the native people who led the attack. But that revolt was just the first of many.

Attacks went on for years up and down the state. Most of them did not improve things. In fact, many times, they made life worse for the native people. Spanish soldiers wanted to keep American Indians from revolting. They used many methods to do this. One of the most common ways was to publicly punish the native people who took part in the revolts.

This photograph shows the remains of Mission San Diego after a fire.

Tile Rooftops

To protect the missions from flaming arrow attacks, the rooftops were changed to tile. The tiles were made from clay and dried in the sun. Then, they were baked in **kilns**. Today, many modern buildings use tile rooftops like the missions.

Fighting Back

Two American Indians led the attack on the San Diego mission. They were tired of not having control over their lives. The men went to nearby villages. They told their stories to the tribes there. Those tribes agreed to help them revolt. By the time of the attack, the two men had gathered over 800 supporters.

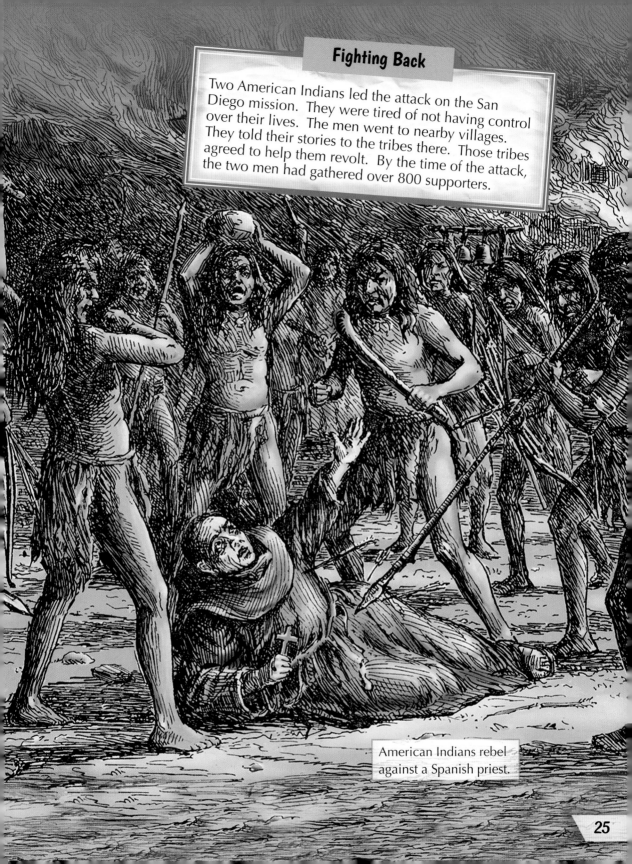

American Indians rebel against a Spanish priest.

Legacy of the Missions

The mission system lasted almost 70 years. It changed when Mexico took control of the area in 1821. Mexican leaders began a plan called **secularization**. This meant that the church would no longer have power or own the land. The land was to go back to the California Indians. But this did not happen. Instead, the new government gave it or sold it to non-natives.

Missions Today

Many of the mission churches are still active. Weddings and funerals are held there. Masses are still performed at some of the missions.

Mission San Juan Capistrano

Gifts from the Missions

Even though there were some bad outcomes from the missions, there were some good as well. The names of many cities come from the missions. The first crops grown at the missions helped improve farming methods in the state. **Stucco** and tiled rooftops on houses were first used on the missions. The freeways and highways were once mission trails. The missions helped define the state of California.

bell marker for El Camino Real

Road Trip

The California missions are host to millions of tourists each year. Luckily, there is an easy way to see them all. Just take the California Missions Trail! This 600-mile (950-kilometer) trek spans most of the state. Buckle up and get comfortable!

Track It!

The Mission Era lasted almost 70 years. By identifying and describing the era's major events, other people can learn about its importance to California and the American Indians.

Create a time line that shows the people, places, and events of this time period. Be sure to include names of people and places where possible.

Mission Santa Barbara

Glossary

belfry—part of a church where the bells are; bell tower

canonized—officially declared a saint by the Roman Catholic Church

climates—the usual weather conditions of places

colonies—areas ruled by a country or countries far away

convert—change from one religion or belief to another

corrals—fenced-in areas to keep animals

founded—built or started

immunities—the body's abilities to fight off infections from diseases

interrelated—connected to one another

kilns—ovens used for hardening, burning, or drying things, such as pottery

marsh—a soft, wet area of land that has many plants

missionaries—people sent by a church to convert others

missions—places or buildings where religious work is done

presidios—walled forts used to protect property

ranchos—Spanish word for *ranches*; large pieces of land

revolts—attempts to end someone's authority

secularization—the act of separating something from a religious connection

stucco—a material that is used to cover the outside walls of houses and buildings

traditions—ways of thinking or doing something that have been done by a particular group for a long time

Index

American Indians, 6, 8, 10, 13, 16, 20–25, 28

Asia, 4

Calafia, 4

California Indians, 6–7, 16, 22, 26, 32

California Missions Trail, 27

Carmel, 11

Christianity, 6, 10, 20

climates, 16

colonies, 4

Columbus, Christopher, 4

Crespí, Juan, 8–9, 32

de Portolá, Gaspar, 9, 12–13

El Camino Real, 12, 27

England, 4

Florida, 8

France, 4

Golden Gate Bridge, 13

hunted/gathered, 21

Mexico, 6, 26

native people, 4, 9, 13, 21–24, 26

Pope John Paul II, 10

Portugal, 4

presidios, 13, 15

pueblos, 15

ranchos, 15

Sacred Expedition, 8, 13, 32

San Diego, 9–10, 24–25, 31

San Francisco, 9–10, 13, 32

San Juan Capistrano, 26

San Luis Obispo, 18

Santa Barbara, 3, 23, 28

Santa Clara, 18–19

Santa Clara University, 19

Serra, Junípero, 9–11, 13, 18–20

Soledad, 16

Spain, 4, 8, 13, 16

Texas, 8

Mission San Diego

Your Turn!

Different Perspectives

During the Sacred Expedition, Father Crespí wrote details about the geography of California. He also noted details about the California Indians and how they lived. The California Indian perspective was not recorded very often.

Imagine you are a California Indian. You live during the Sacred Expedition in the San Francisco Bay area. Look at the Spanish soldiers and missionaries in the painting. As a California Indian, what do you first think and feel? What are you curious about? Write a detailed journal entry about that first sighting.